World War II and the Cold War

1940–1960

SADDLEBACK
EDUCATIONAL PUBLISHING

Saddleback's *Graphic American History*

3 7548 00029 3758

SADDLEBACK
EDUCATIONAL PUBLISHING
www.sdlback.com

Copyright © 2009, 2010 by Saddleback Educational Publishing
All rights reserved. No part of this book may be reproduced in any form
or by any means, electronic or mechanical, including photocopying,
recording, or by any information storage and retrieval system, without the
written permission of the publisher.

ISBN-13: 978-1-59905-366-0
ISBN-10: 1-59905-366-7
eBook: 978-1-60291-694-4

Printed in Guangzhou, China
0712/CA21200995

16 15 14 13 12   4 5 6 7 8 9 10 11

America at last!

In 1620, it took the Pilgrims more than nine weeks to cross the Atlantic in the *Mayflower*.

In 1927, Charles Lindbergh flew from New York to Paris in 33 hours.

Because of the slowness of communication, the Battle of New Orleans was fought two weeks after the War of 1812 had ended.

Roosevelt and Secretary of State Hull wanted to improve our relations with our Latin American neighbors.

They have had good reason in the past to distrust our intentions.

We must convince them that we are no longer "big brother" trying to tell them what to do.

In 1934, our marines were withdrawn from Haiti, ending 19 years of military domination by the United States.

The United States surrendered the rights of intervention in Haiti and Nicaragua, given it by treaty. In 1936, it surrendered its treaty right to intervene in the Panama Republic.

At the Pan-American Conference at Montevideo, Secretary Hull approved a new doctrine.

No state has the right to intervene in the internal or external affairs of another.

In 1940, the 21 republics of the Inter-American Conference met in Havana.

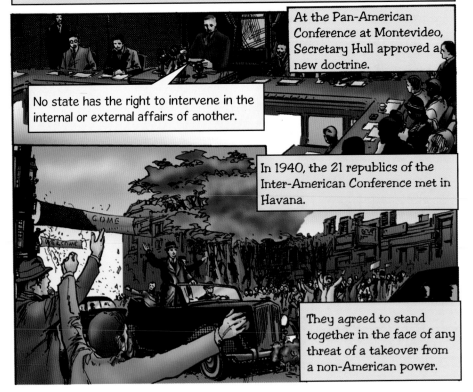

They agreed to stand together in the face of any threat of a takeover from a non-American power.

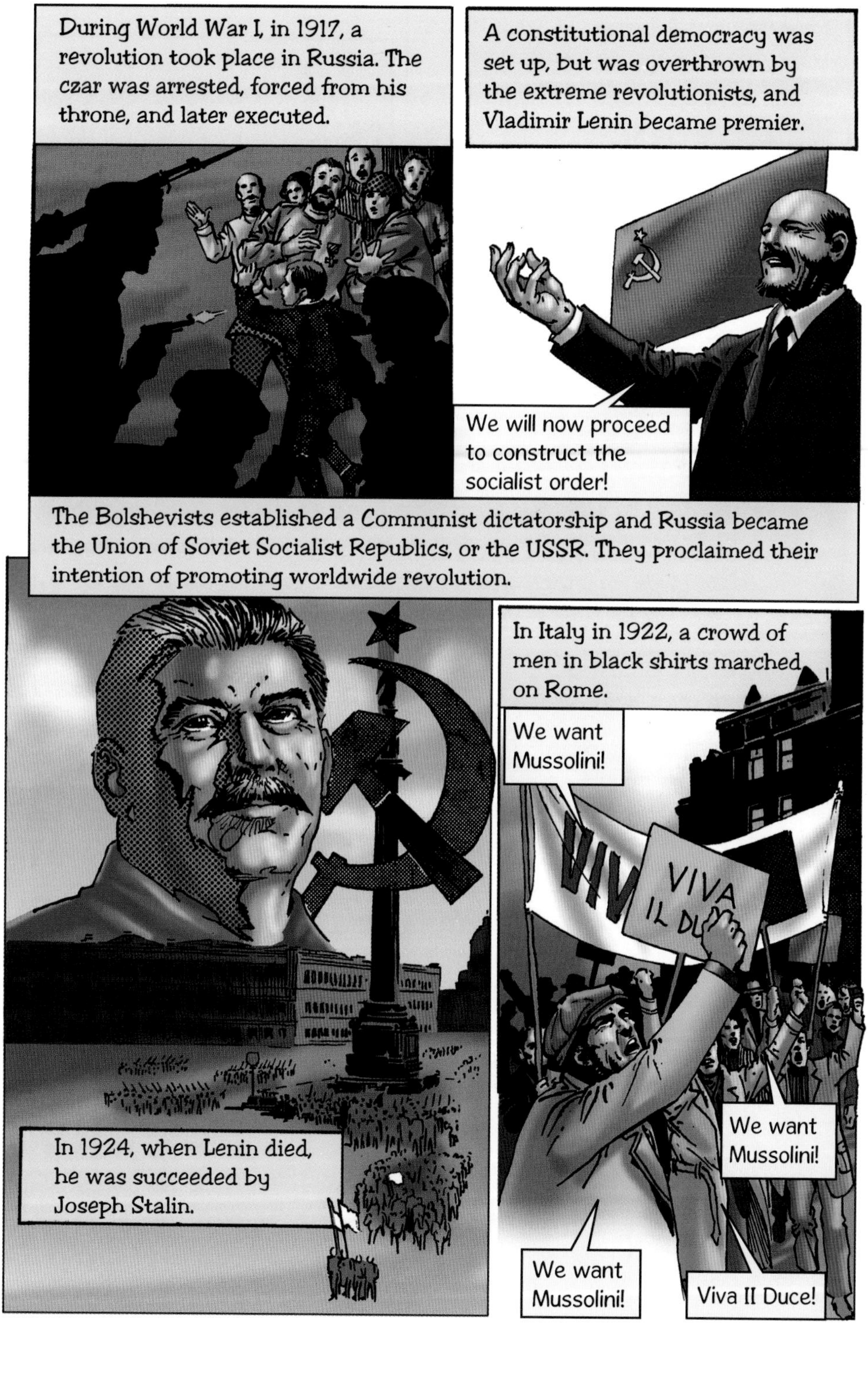
During World War I, in 1917, a revolution took place in Russia. The czar was arrested, forced from his throne, and later executed.
A constitutional democracy was set up, but was overthrown by the extreme revolutionists, and Vladimir Lenin became premier.
We will now proceed to construct the socialist order!
The Bolshevists established a Communist dictatorship and Russia became the Union of Soviet Socialist Republics, or the USSR. They proclaimed their intention of promoting worldwide revolution.
In 1924, when Lenin died, he was succeeded by Joseph Stalin.
In Italy in 1922, a crowd of men in black shirts marched on Rome.
We want Mussolini!
VIVA
We want Mussolini!
We want Mussolini!
Viva Il Duce!

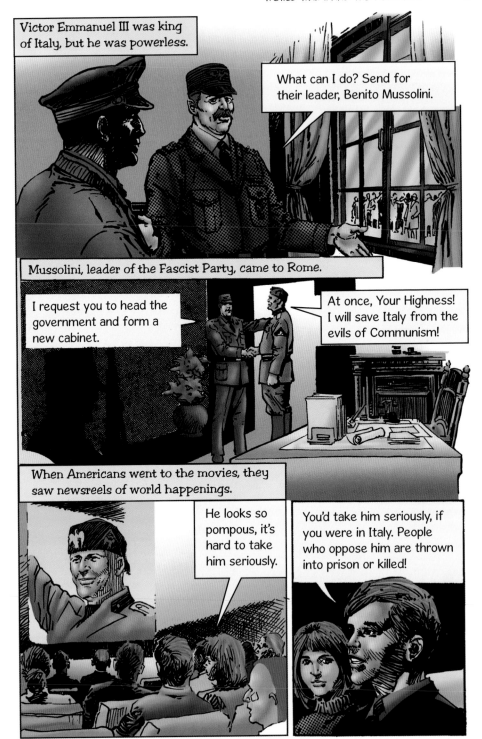

Victor Emmanuel III was king of Italy, but he was powerless.

What can I do? Send for their leader, Benito Mussolini.

Mussolini, leader of the Fascist Party, came to Rome.

I request you to head the government and form a new cabinet.

At once, Your Highness! I will save Italy from the evils of Communism!

When Americans went to the movies, they saw newsreels of world happenings.

He looks so pompous, it's hard to take him seriously.

You'd take him seriously, if you were in Italy. People who oppose him are thrown into prison or killed!

In a few years, newsreels also showed Mussolini's son-in-law, Count Ciano, head of the Italian air force.

In 1935, Ciano led bombing raids against native tribesmen in Ethiopia.

An Italian army marched across Ethiopia to the capital, Addis Ababa, strafing, gassing, and shelling as they went.

Fleeing the country, its emperor, Haile Selassie, appealed to the League of Nations for help.

But the League was powerless, and Italy took over Ethiopia.

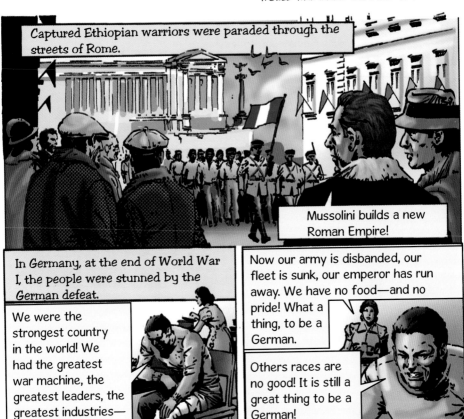

Captured Ethiopian warriors were paraded through the streets of Rome.

Mussolini builds a new Roman Empire!

In Germany, at the end of World War I, the people were stunned by the German defeat.

We were the strongest country in the world! We had the greatest war machine, the greatest leaders, the greatest industries—how could we lose the war?

Now our army is disbanded, our fleet is sunk, our emperor has run away. We have no food—and no pride! What a thing, to be a German.

Others races are no good! It is still a great thing to be a German!

People began to listen to a hypnotic young speaker and politician.

Who is he?

His name is Adolph Hitler.

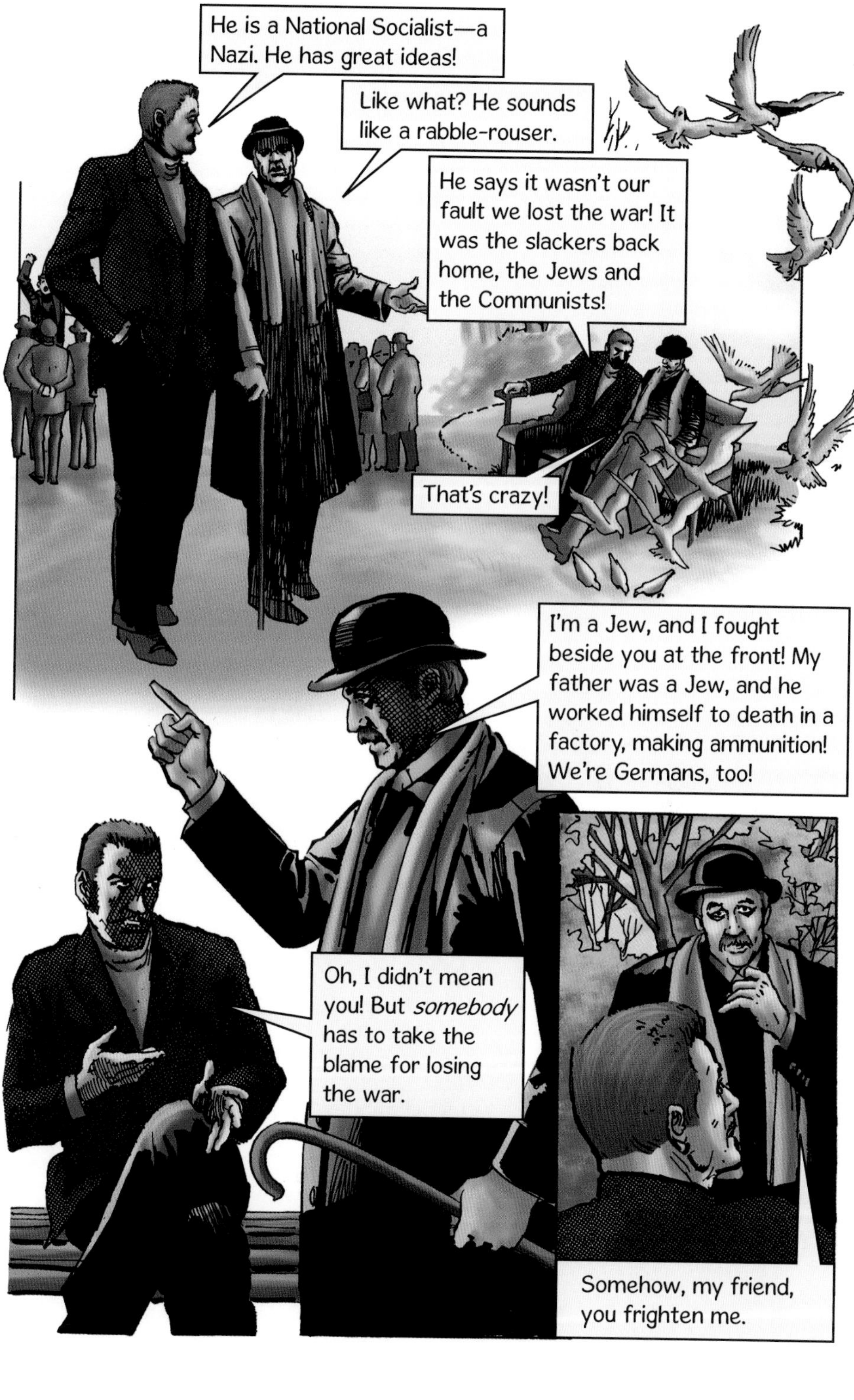
He is a National Socialist—a Nazi. He has great ideas!
Like what? He sounds like a rabble-rouser.
He says it wasn't our fault we lost the war! It was the slackers back home, the Jews and the Communists!
That's crazy!
I'm a Jew, and I fought beside you at the front! My father was a Jew, and he worked himself to death in a factory, making ammunition! We're Germans, too!
Oh, I didn't mean you! But *somebody* has to take the blame for losing the war.
Somehow, my friend, you frighten me.

Using a combination of force, trickery, and oratory, by 1933 Adolph Hitler controlled the German government. He persuaded the aged President von Hindenburg to sign a special decree.

For the protection of the people and the state.

This suspends civil liberties and legalizes all Nazi actions in putting down rival political parties!

Heil Hitler!

Within a brief time, Hitler became the absolute dictator of Germany, abolishing all civil liberties, persecuting the Christian churches, hounding the Jews, imprisoning or murdering many, and confiscating their property. Then he turned toward the outside world.

I will tear up the Versailles Treaty, build a mighty military machine, and Germany will become Lord of the Earth! It is all here in my book! If they don't want to believe it, so much the worse for them.

Mein Kampf (My Struggle) was a book written by Hitler in which he set forth his ideas and his ambitions to conquer the world.

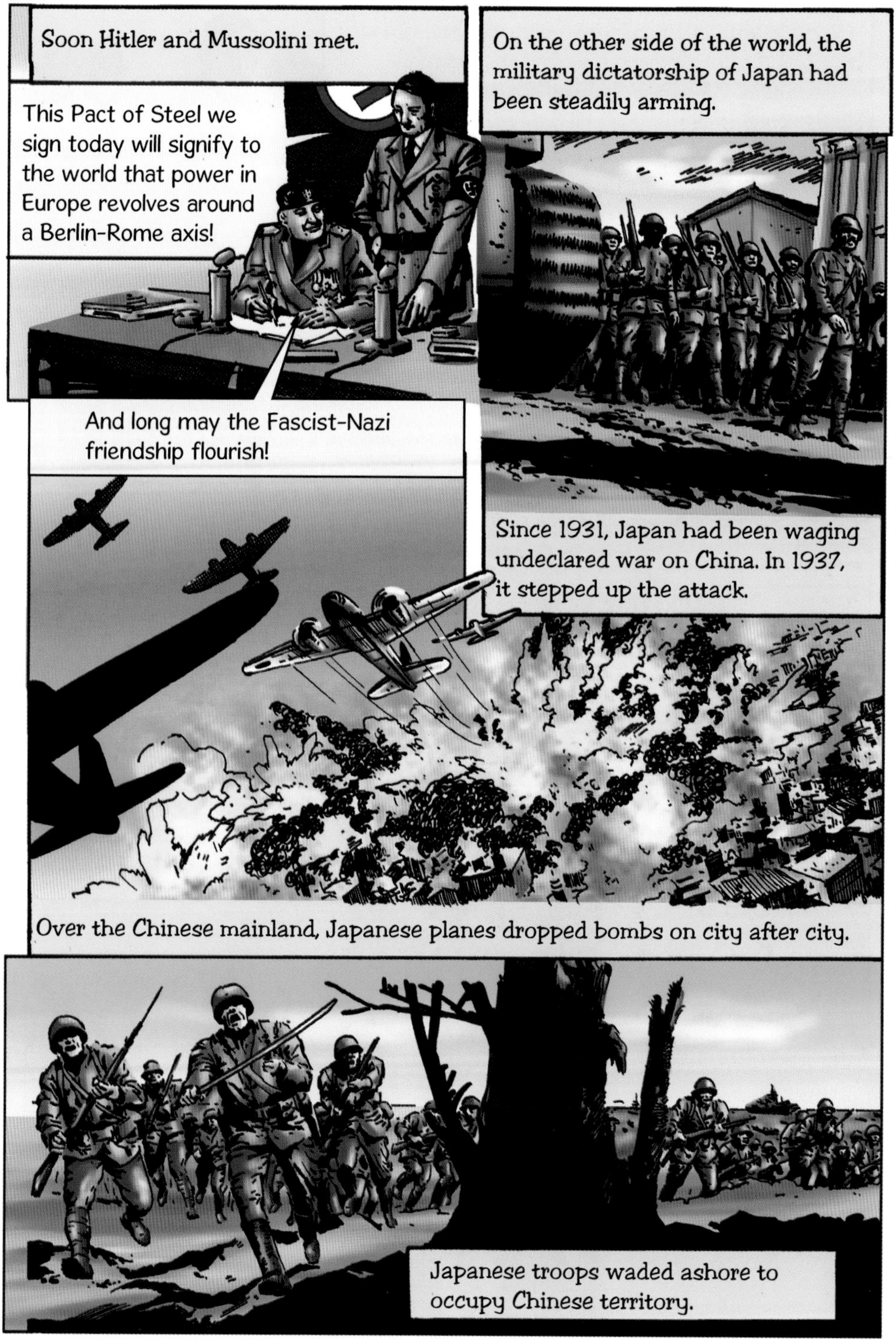
Soon Hitler and Mussolini met.
This Pact of Steel we sign today will signify to the world that power in Europe revolves around a Berlin-Rome axis!
And long may the Fascist-Nazi friendship flourish!
On the other side of the world, the military dictatorship of Japan had been steadily arming.
Since 1931, Japan had been waging undeclared war on China. In 1937, it stepped up the attack.
Over the Chinese mainland, Japanese planes dropped bombs on city after city.
Japanese troops waded ashore to occupy Chinese territory.

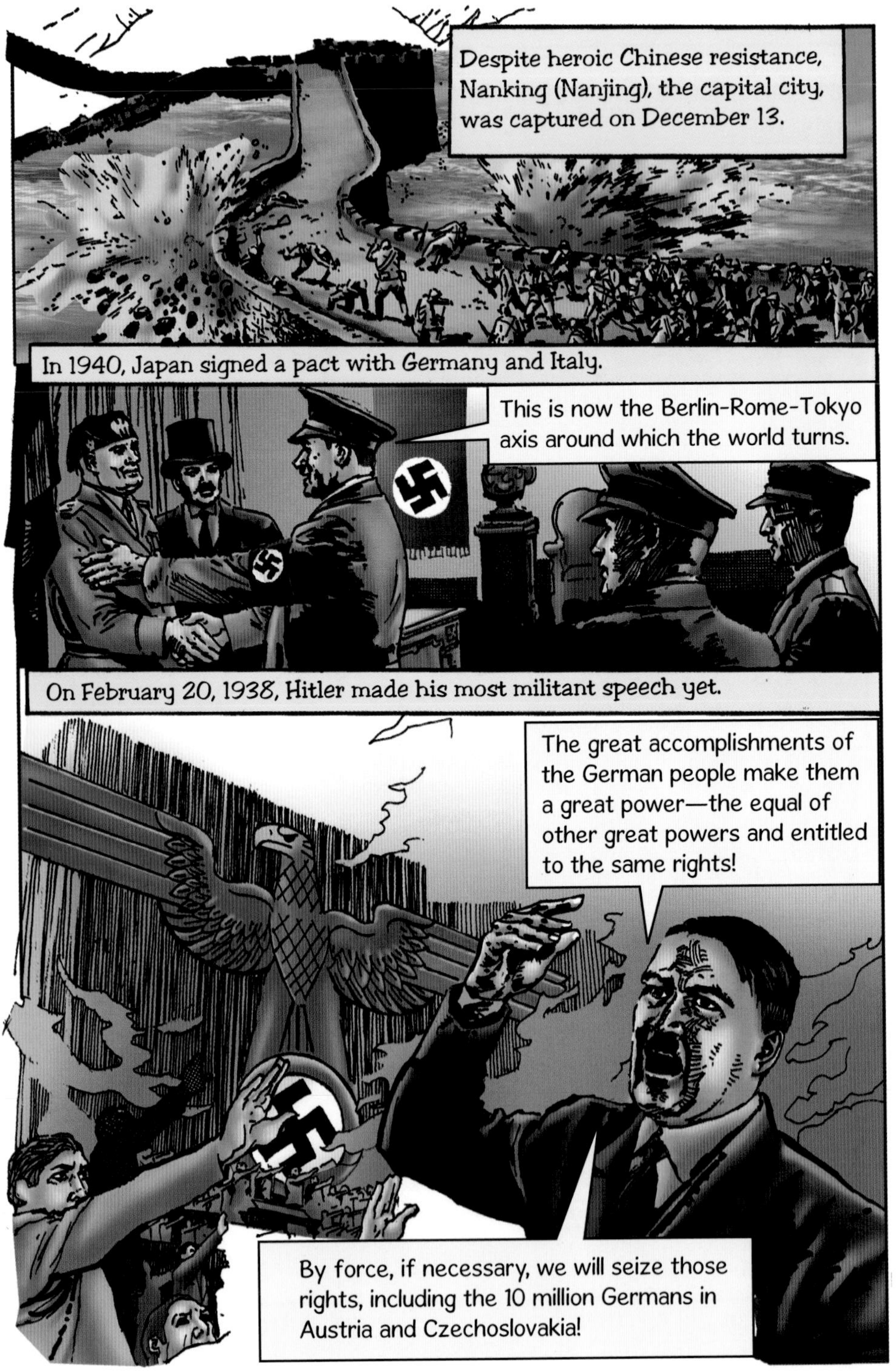
Despite heroic Chinese resistance, Nanking (Nanjing), the capital city, was captured on December 13.
In 1940, Japan signed a pact with Germany and Italy.
This is now the Berlin-Rome-Tokyo axis around which the world turns.
On February 20, 1938, Hitler made his most militant speech yet.
The great accomplishments of the German people make them a great power—the equal of other great powers and entitled to the same rights!
By force, if necessary, we will seize those rights, including the 10 million Germans in Austria and Czechoslovakia!

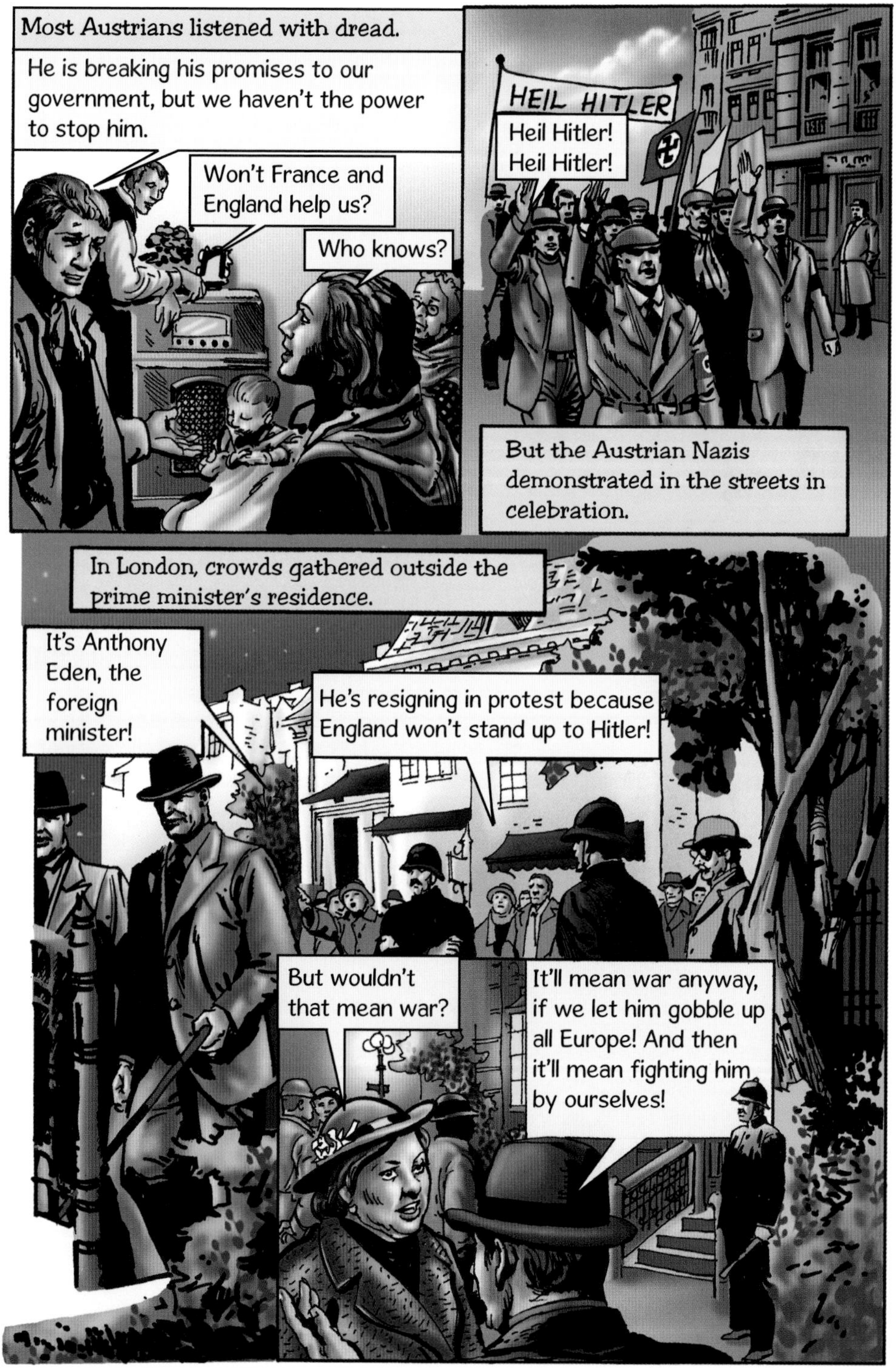
Most Austrians listened with dread.
He is breaking his promises to our government, but we haven't the power to stop him.
Won't France and England help us?
Who knows?
HEIL HITLER
Heil Hitler! Heil Hitler!
But the Austrian Nazis demonstrated in the streets in celebration.
In London, crowds gathered outside the prime minister's residence.
It's Anthony Eden, the foreign minister!
He's resigning in protest because England won't stand up to Hitler!
But wouldn't that mean war?
It'll mean war anyway, if we let him gobble up all Europe! And then it'll mean fighting him by ourselves!

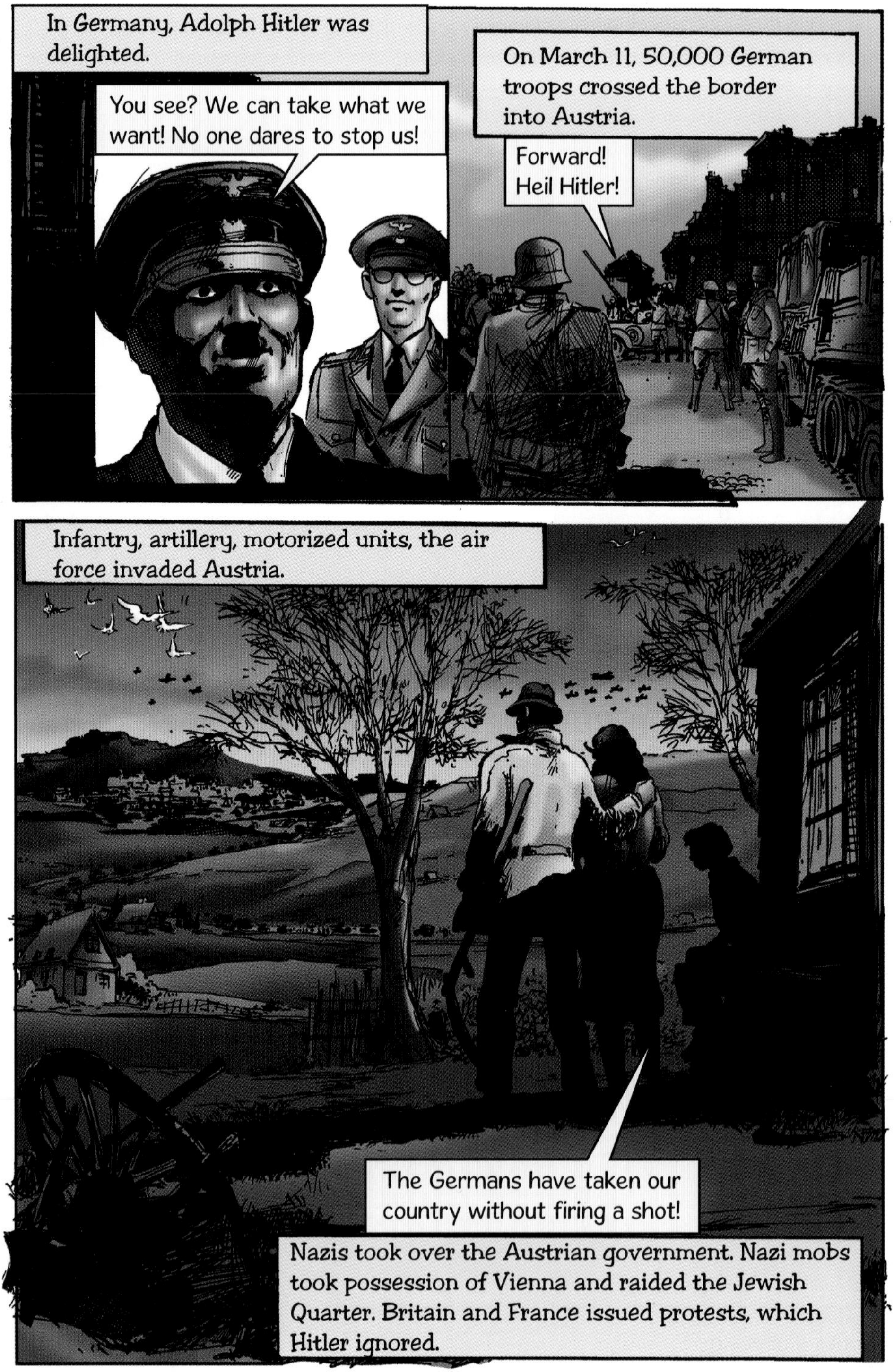
In Germany, Adolph Hitler was delighted.
You see? We can take what we want! No one dares to stop us!
On March 11, 50,000 German troops crossed the border into Austria.
Forward! Heil Hitler!
Infantry, artillery, motorized units, the air force invaded Austria.
The Germans have taken our country without firing a shot!
Nazis took over the Austrian government. Nazi mobs took possession of Vienna and raided the Jewish Quarter. Britain and France issued protests, which Hitler ignored.

Czechoslovakia was the one remaining republic in Europe east of the Rhine. When Hitler threatened to take the country, the Czechs were determined to fight, relying on the help of Great Britain and France. But once again they refused to fight, and Hitler took over Czechoslovakia.

Then Hitler threatened Poland. Sir Neville Henderson, British ambassador to Germany delivered a letter to Hitler.

Sir, have you considered the contents of the prime minister's letter?

His protests are nonsense! Britain has no business in eastern Europe! Your support merely encourages a hopeless Polish resistance.

The same day in Moscow, the German von Ribbentrop and the Russian Premier Molotov signed a pact of non-aggression.

To many years of friendship between our two great nations!

Heil Hitler!

The German ambassador to Great Britain reported to Hitler.

The British lion is stuffed, not real! They will not fight!

But this time there was no choice. Hitler had to be stopped somewhere. The British ordered war ships concentrated in the Skagerrak.

France called up her reserves.

At dawn, German planes began the bombardment of Polish cities.

On Sunday, September 3, 1939, the British prime minister broadcast to the world.

I have to tell you that this country is at war with Germany. France is joining Britain in fulfillment of her pledges to Poland.

Children were evacuated from English cities.

Three million of them! Poor little tots.

Better than leaving 'em here for Hitler to bomb!

American tourists in Europe hurried for home. Three hundred were on the *Athenia* on September 4 when it was torpedoed and sunk.

The French manned their great Maginot Line fortifications.

In American the big news was the newly opened New York World's Fair. Six hundred thousand people were there on opening day.

The Trylon and Perisphere set the theme.

A Japanese Shinto shrine made of diamonds and pearls enclosed a copy of the Liberty Bell.

People watched a new development called television.

Do you suppose it'll ever be practical for homes?

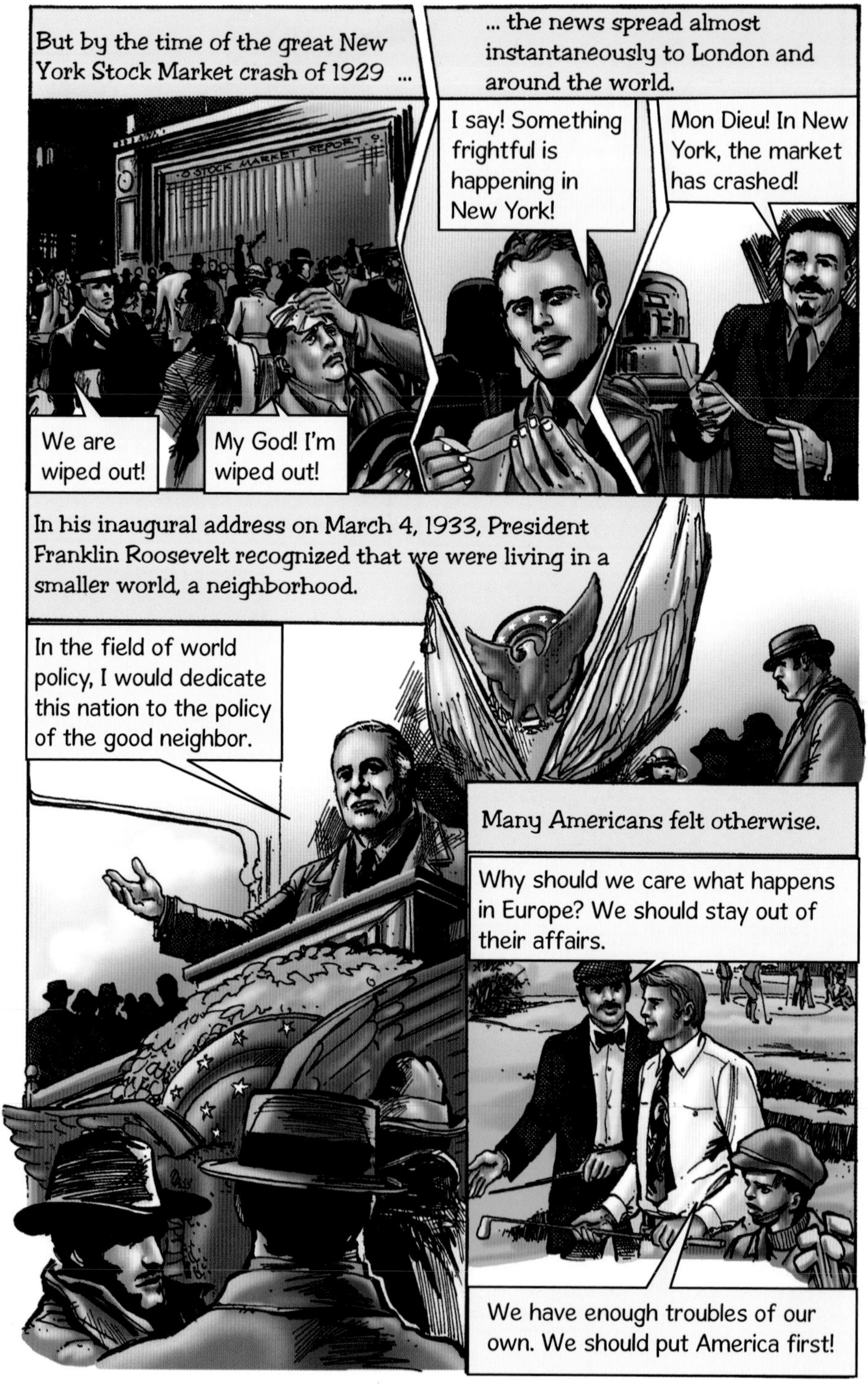
But by the time of the great New York Stock Market crash of 1929 ...
STOCK MARKET REPORT
We are wiped out!
My God! I'm wiped out!
... the news spread almost instantaneously to London and around the world.
I say! Something frightful is happening in New York!
Mon Dieu! In New York, the market has crashed!
In his inaugural address on March 4, 1933, President Franklin Roosevelt recognized that we were living in a smaller world, a neighborhood.
In the field of world policy, I would dedicate this nation to the policy of the good neighbor.
Many Americans felt otherwise.
Why should we care what happens in Europe? We should stay out of their affairs.
We have enough troubles of our own. We should put America first!

During the 1930s Americans did not want to get involved in Europe.

We've got enough to worry about, trying to get through the Depression.

We fought to save the world for democracy in World War I, and look at it now!

In 1935, Congress passed a neutrality act forbidding the sale of munitions to either side engaged in a war.

In May 1940, Britain had a new leader, as Winston Churchill succeeded Chamberlain.

The Germans invaded Denmark, pouring ashore from ships in the harbor and overrunning the country in one day.

I have nothing to offer but blood, toil, tears, and sweat. What is our aim? Victory!

In snowbound Norway, they quickly overcame Norwegians and their British reinforcements.

In Oslo, Norway, they commandeered city bus drivers to move German troops.

The first three drivers drove their Nazi troops over a cliff.

Heil on board here!

The Germans stopped using Oslo bus drivers.

In May, the Germans smashed their way through the Netherlands and Belgium and into France, giving the world a demonstration of Nazi "blitzkrieg" or "lightning war."

Tanks and armored divisions rushed the frontier bridges.

Paratroopers landing behind the enemy lines destroyed bridges, factories, railways.

The Luftwaffe—the German air force—laid waste to airfields and harbors and destroyed Rotterdam.

Dive bombers attacked enemy troops in a way unknown to warfare before.

They also bombed or strafed with machine-gun fire the thousands of refugees fleeing across France ahead of the German armies.

On June 14, the Nazis entered Paris.

Americans were stunned to hear of the surrender of France.

France has fallen? One of the world's greatest armies beaten in six weeks? Impossible!

The Germans couldn't reach Paris in four years of fighting in World War I.

Maybe Hitler really is going to conquer the world.

Now England's alone. I suppose he'll invade England next.

Mussolini spoke to cheering thousands in Rome.

The Italian government has declared war on Great Britain and France, to take effect at one minute after midnight.

So another large army was added to Hitler's force.

President Roosevelt spoke at the University of Virginia.

The hand that held the dagger has plunged it into the back of its neighbor. It is an obvious delusion that we can safely permit the United States to become a lone island in a world dominated by force.

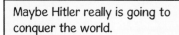

The surrender of the French army left the British army in a trap in France.

Our backs are to the Channel coast. German forces are closing in from every side.

We must retreat to the sea, trusting the navy to get us away, and fighting a withdrawal action all the way.

There is no way for supplies of food and ammunition to reach us.

The navy was ready with every available naval vessel. But with the great pressure of the German advance, it seemed impossible to evacuate the men in time. The seafaring English people rose to the emergency, using every sort of vessel that would float.

Lifeboats, speedboats, rowboats, yachts, fishing boats, fireboats, tugs—all joined the fleet, manned by amateur sailors.

All right, lad. We've off for Dunkirk.

At Dunkirk, the Germans battered the sea and the beaches with shells from the land and bombs from the air.

It went on for nine days. 338,226 men of the Allied forces were brought back to England in the most remarkable evacuation in history.

22

In the House of Commons, Churchill spoke.

We shall defend our island. We shall fight on the beaches, we shall fight in the fields and in the streets. We shall never surrender!

The American people wanted to help England, but not to fight. Roosevelt had a plan.

I have ordered the transfer of 50 over-age American destroyers to Great Britain. In return we will receive sea and air bases at eight strategic points.

These bases will create a new American defense line removed from our shores, making sea and air attacks upon us more difficult if not impossible.

Congress passed a selective service and training bill, the country's first peace-time draft law.

Hitler planned to invade England, but first the RAF, the English air force, had to be destroyed. He gave orders to Goering, commander of the Luftwaffe.

Send bombers to lure out the British fighters. Then shoot them down!

I will gain air supremacy in four days, and destroy the RAF in a month.

Every day more than 1,000 German bombers, escorted by fighter planes, appeared in waves over England.

Their particular targets were airfields, aircraft factories, and radar stations.

Radar gave the English pilots four minutes' warning. In three minutes they were airborne.

Along the Channel cliffs, the English watched the aerial combats and the damaged planes spiralling to the sea.

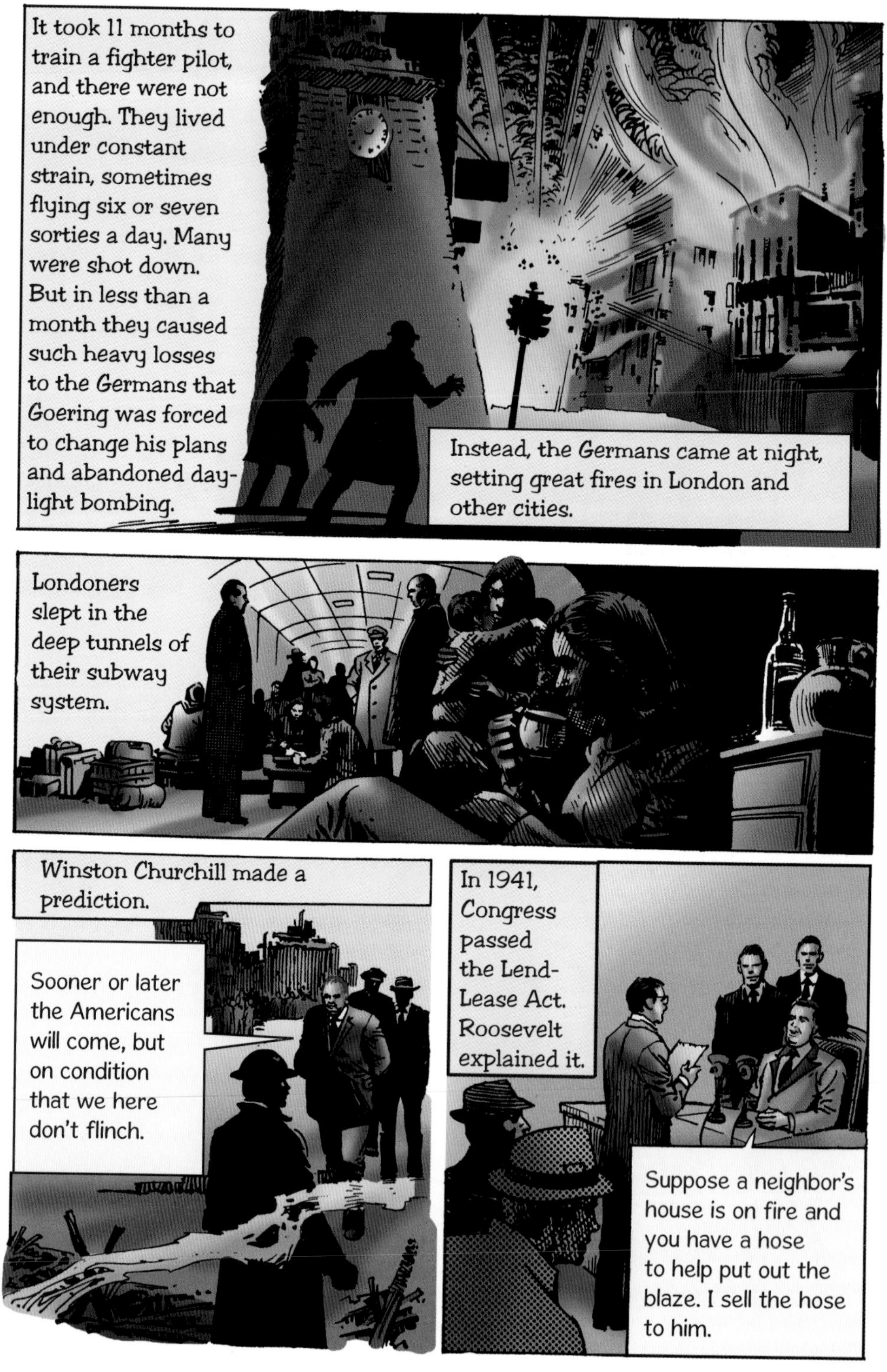
It took 11 months to train a fighter pilot, and there were not enough. They lived under constant strain, sometimes flying six or seven sorties a day. Many were shot down. But in less than a month they caused such heavy losses to the Germans that Goering was forced to change his plans and abandoned daylight bombing.
Instead, the Germans came at night, setting great fires in London and other cities.
Londoners slept in the deep tunnels of their subway system.
Winston Churchill made a prediction.
Sooner or later the Americans will come, but on condition that we here don't flinch.
In 1941, Congress passed the Lend-Lease Act. Roosevelt explained it.
Suppose a neighbor's house is on fire and you have a hose to help put out the blaze. I sell the hose to him.

What I am trying to do is eliminate the dollar sign. We will speed aid to Britain in every way short of war.

And in burning London, Winston Churchill said ...

Give us the tools, and we will finish the job.

In the 1930s Japan had grown increasingly militaristic and aggressive. She annexed Korea in 1910, Manchuria in 1932, and invaded China in 1937. In 1938, she announced the creation of a Greater East-Asia Co-Prosperity Sphere, making it obvious that Japan intended to control that part of the world.

In mid-November, 1941, a Japanese strike force of aircraft carriers, battleships, cruisers, and destroyers rendezvoused in the Pacific.

On December 2, Admiral Yamamoto broadcast the code for PROCEED WITH ATTACK.

Climb Mount Niitaka!

In the dark dawn hours of Sunday, December 7, 1941, torpedo planes, bombers, and fighters soared off the carrier flight-decks.

An hour later, the planes broke out of the clouds above a peaceful Pearl Harbor.

On the island, some people were on the way to early church services.

On the American ships, sailors were sleeping, breakfasting, or taking it easy.

Planes? Must be an air raid drill.

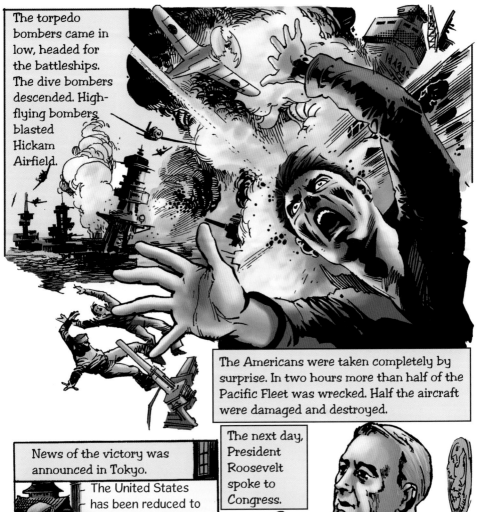

The torpedo bombers came in low, headed for the battleships. The dive bombers descended. High-flying bombers blasted Hickam Airfield.

The Americans were taken completely by surprise. In two hours more than half of the Pacific Fleet was wrecked. Half the aircraft were damaged and destroyed.

The next day, President Roosevelt spoke to Congress.

Yesterday, a day which will live in infamy, the United States was suddenly and deliberately attacked by naval and air forces of the Empire of Japan.

News of the victory was announced in Tokyo.

The United States has been reduced to a third class power. *Banzai!*

Last night Japanese forces attacked Hong Kong, Guam, the Philippine Islands, Wake Island, and Midway Island.

Congress voted an immediate declaration of war against Japan.

Three days later Germany and Italy declared war on the United States. American draft boards were swamped with volunteers.

ENLIST NOW

Women enlisted in the Army WACs, the Navy WAVEs, and the Coast Guard SPARs.

Factories worked day and night shifts to supply war materials.

If it isn't Rosie the Riveter!

Herman Goering, commander of the Luftwaffe, laughed at the Americans.

Americans can't build planes, only iceboxes and razor blades.

But in 1944, American workers turned out 96,000 planes.

In February 1942, a Japanese submarine surfaced off the California coast and fired shells inland.

They caused no casualties, but people were frightened.

Japanese—right out there—firing on us! What's to stop them killing us next time?

This led to a different kind of alarm.

I saw some funny lights up there last night—like signals!

Do you think Japanese spies were signaling to a sub?

When I was in a radio shop the other day, there was a Japanese man buying shortwave radio equipment!

May be we should report all this to the authorities. There are so many Japanese in California!

The spy scare, and pressure from California officials on federal authorities, led to the forcible evacuation of 110,000 Japanese, aliens and citizens alike, from the West coast to the interior of the country, where they were kept in detention camps for the duration of the war.

At the time the decision was made, the Japanese were sweeping everything before them in the Pacific. No one seemed to realize how unjustly Japanese Americans were being treated.

But many Japanese Americans enlisted, and the Japanese-American 442nd Regiment was the most decorated in the American army.

Sergeant Nagano, for conspicuous bravery under enemy fire ...

When American industries geared up for defense production, African Americans found themselves excluded.

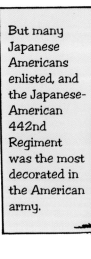

HELP WANTED WHITE ONLY

African-American leaders like A. Philip Randolph expressed their resentment.

Of 30,000 defense workers in New York City, only 142 are black. Many plants will not hire black workers.

And the few they do hire are elevator operators and janitors.

Randolph, Walter White of the NAACP, and T. Arnold Hill of the Urban League conferred.

The Draft Act requires blacks to serve in the armed forces—but we're segregated in the army, limited to mess duty in the navy, and not allowed at all in the air corps and marines.

We must draw up a memorandum to the president urging our acceptance on the basis of ability, not race.

The memorandum was sent, but nothing changed.

The government won't act until it sees 10, 20, maybe 50,000 African Americans on the White House lawn. A march on Washington, that's what we need. Let's go!

In June 1941, leaders of African-American organizations had an announcement to make.

On July 1, A. Philip Randolph, Walter White, Adam Clayton Powell Jr., and Frank Crosswaith will lead a Washington protest march.

We'll go! Count on us!

President Roosevelt called the march leaders to Washington.

I ask you to postpone your demands, in the interest of nation and security.

Mr. President, since the earliest days of our nation we have fought its wars—and postponed our demands. We cannot call off this march.

On June 25, 1941, Roosevelt signed Executive Order No. 8802, the Fair Employment Practices Act.

This act bans discrimination in defense plants, government offices, and the services, because of race, creed, or national origin.

Since it had already achieved its objective, the the march on Washington did not take place.

It's the first time since Lincoln signed the Emancipation Proclamation that a president has acted to protect the civil rights of black people.

It shows the value of a nonviolent demonstration.

Because of the war, great amounts of food and other supplies were needed for our troops and our allies. Scarcities developed.

No canned peaches? I never heard of such a thing!

Don't you know there's a war on?

An Office of Price Administration—the OPA—was set up. It set prices for scarce items, and issued ration stamps to distribute them fairly.

Then you can't buy any!

The blue stamps are for sugar and the red stamps are for fats—butter and so on.

Suppose I run out of stamps?

Meat, fats, sugar, coffee, gasoline, fuel oil, rubber, all were in short supply. Ceiling prices were set on wages, rents, and many prices, to prevent runaway inflation.

With gasoline and tires hard to come by, many people disposed of their cars.

We'll buy war-bonds, and then use the money for a new car after the war.

From 1941 to 1945, government bond sales amounted to more than $61 billion!

Between the war supplies pouring from American factories and the fighting fronts were the Atlantic Ocean and German submarines and planes!

Cargo ships were gathered together in convoys, with naval vessels to protect them.

There are 37 ships, sir, and two escort vessels.

Very well, we will proceed at the speed of the slowest vessel.

The convoy would sail in secrecy, under strict blackout conditions.

A high-flying German scout plane was a bad sign.

She's German all right.

She'll radio our position to the nearest sub pack. Prepare for action!

The German submarines attacked in packs, catching the ships when they made ideal targets silhouetted against a rising or setting sun.

Torpedo, port bow!

In the first seven months of 1942, German subs sank 681 Allied ships, with few losses themselves. That summer, one heavily escorted convoy lost 22 out of 33 cargo ships. But somehow, some of the supplies got through. New scientific developments, most importantly radar and sonar, began to counteract the submarine threat. Though German submarines fought to the last, by 1943, the Battle of the Atlantic was essentially won.

In early 1942, the news was all bad.

The Japanese have taken the Philippines. They're threatening Australia!

German subs have sunk ships right in Chesapeake Bay!

And the Germans are raining bombs down on English cities!

But Americans were learning to fight modern wars, and were building a new type of war ship.

It's an aircraft carrier—like a floating airfield! Now we can carry an aerial war to the Japanese!

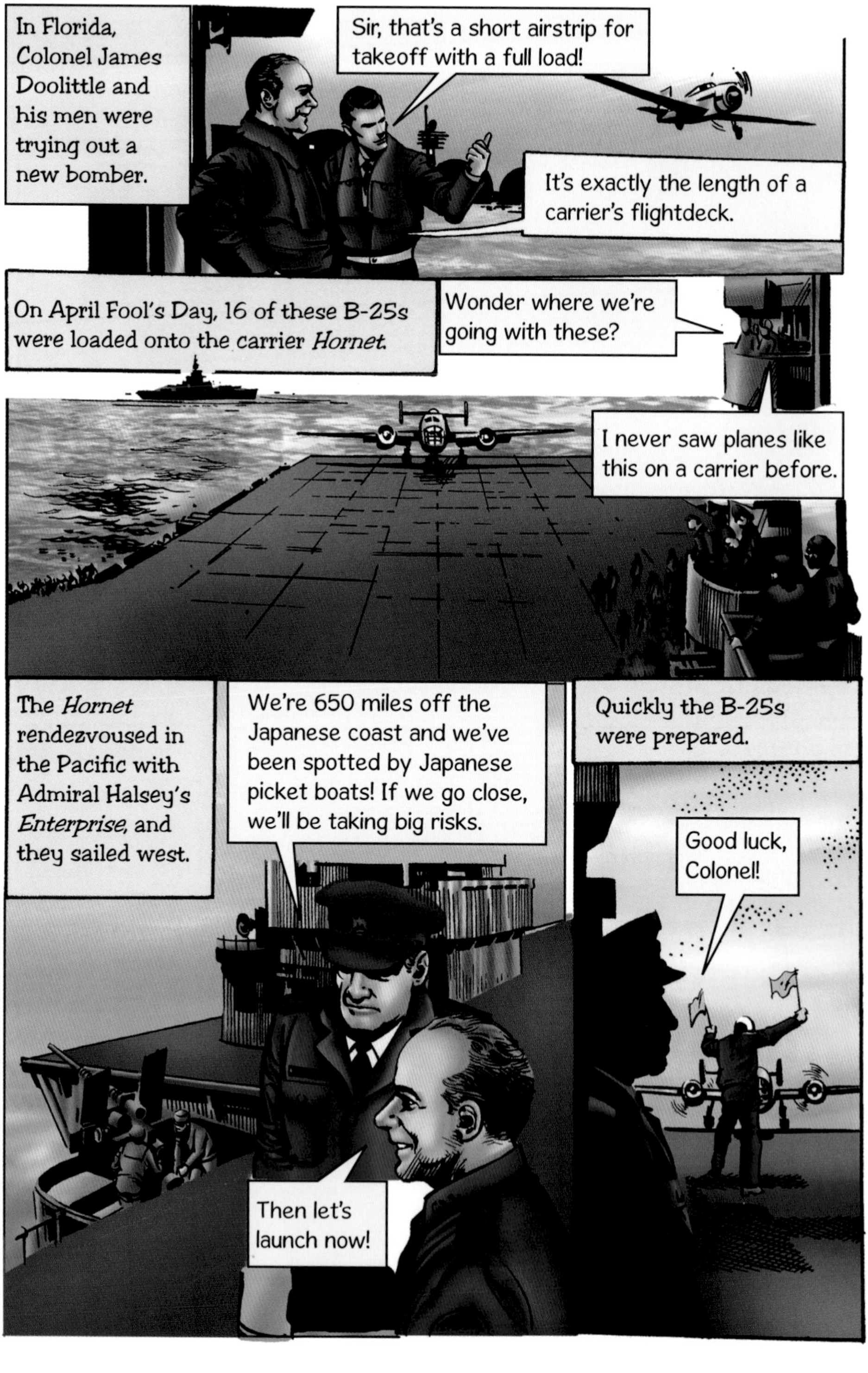
In Florida, Colonel James Doolittle and his men were trying out a new bomber.
Sir, that's a short airstrip for takeoff with a full load!
It's exactly the length of a carrier's flightdeck.
On April Fool's Day, 16 of these B-25s were loaded onto the carrier *Hornet*.
Wonder where we're going with these?
I never saw planes like this on a carrier before.
The *Hornet* rendezvoused in the Pacific with Admiral Halsey's *Enterprise*, and they sailed west.
We're 650 miles off the Japanese coast and we've been spotted by Japanese picket boats! If we go close, we'll be taking big risks.
Then let's launch now!
Quickly the B-25s were prepared.
Good luck, Colonel!

Tensely, men watched the launch. Waves were breaking over the carrier deck. The army pilots had never flown off a flattop before.

But they all made it. Four hours later, bombs were falling on Tokyo.

Bombs away, men!

The raid did little damage physically, but much damage psychologically.

And the American people were happy.

It's impossible! They told us we could not possibly be bombed!

Perhaps other things they tell us are not true.

At last we've given them something for Pearl Harbor!

Since Pearl Harbor, the Japanese navy had destroyed many American battleships at small cost.

The Imperial Navy is invincible! We must invade Australia and India!

But the Americans cannot be allowed to bomb Japan! Obviously, the bombs came from Midway Island! We must first capture Midway and destroy the American fleet.

The most powerful invasion fleet in Japanese history moved toward Midway Island, an outpost of the Hawaiian Islands.

We are launching a small attack against the Aleutian Islands. The Americans will rush their fleet there, leaving Midway undefended.

But the Americans had broken the Japanese secret radio code.

Sir, the latest Japanese orders.

Word was flashed to Washington.

Flying Fortress bombers ready for Europe, went to Hawaii instead.

Battleships steamed from San Francisco.

The carriers *Enterprise* and *Hornet* took their stations east of Midway.

The battle began on June 4, when Japanese planes flew off their carriers to attack Midway.

But American torpedo planes and dive bombers found the Japanese carriers.

Four Japanese carriers were lost, and their planes landed helplessly in the sea.

The Battle of Midway raged for four days. Then Yamamoto withdrew with the remains of his fleet. The Japanese lost four carriers, a heavy cruiser, and many planes. The Americans lost one carrier, a destroyer and 100 planes. For the first time the Japanese navy, with superior strength, had been beaten. There were many bitter battles still to come, but Midway marked the turning of the tide against the Japanese in the central Pacific.

The non-aggression pact between Nazi Germany and Communist Russia came to an end on June 22, 1941, when Hitler attacked the USSR with the most powerful army the world had ever seen.

German divisions poured into Russia across a 2,000-mile front, crushing the Red Army, advancing 750 miles in two weeks.

Hitler gave orders.

Live off the land! No food need be left for the Russian civilians. Those too old or weak to work may be left to die. Those strong enough must labor for us. In two months we will crush Russia!

On July 3, Stalin, the Russian leader, announced a "scorched earth" policy.

Brothers and sisters, defend our homeland. Leave nothing behind which can help the enemy.

Food supplies and crops were burned. Railroads, bridges, and buildings were destroyed. The Germans advanced across a wasteland.

The Germans advanced to within sight of Moscow. They captured or killed hundreds of thousands of Russian troops. But still there was a Russian army ahead of them. And then a new enemy struck—the Russian winter.

In summer uniforms, the Germans froze in the Russian cold and snow.

The dark colors made them good targets. Russian troops wore warm, white winter suits.

The German high command protested to Hitler.

The German army is not equipped for winter. I strongly advise that we withdraw.

Nonsense! You are dismissed! I will take sole command of the army!

With America at war, people got out maps and followed campaigns.

Mussolini invaded Africa here. Hitler sent in his Afrika Korps under General Rommel, to help, and they were threatening to take the Suez Canal and the Arabian oil fields. And that's when the British 8th Army under General Montgomery attacked at El Alamein and drove them back.

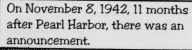

But the fight isn't over yet.

On November 8, 1942, 11 months after Pearl Harbor, there was an announcement.

American troops are reported to be landing on the African coast, under the commander of General Dwight Eisenhower.

For the first time the American army was to give fighting support to the Allies.

Wow! It's the second front!

It's supposed to help Russia, by forcing the Germans to withdraw men and equipment from their Russian front to use on this new front.

I wonder if any of the soldiers are young men we know.

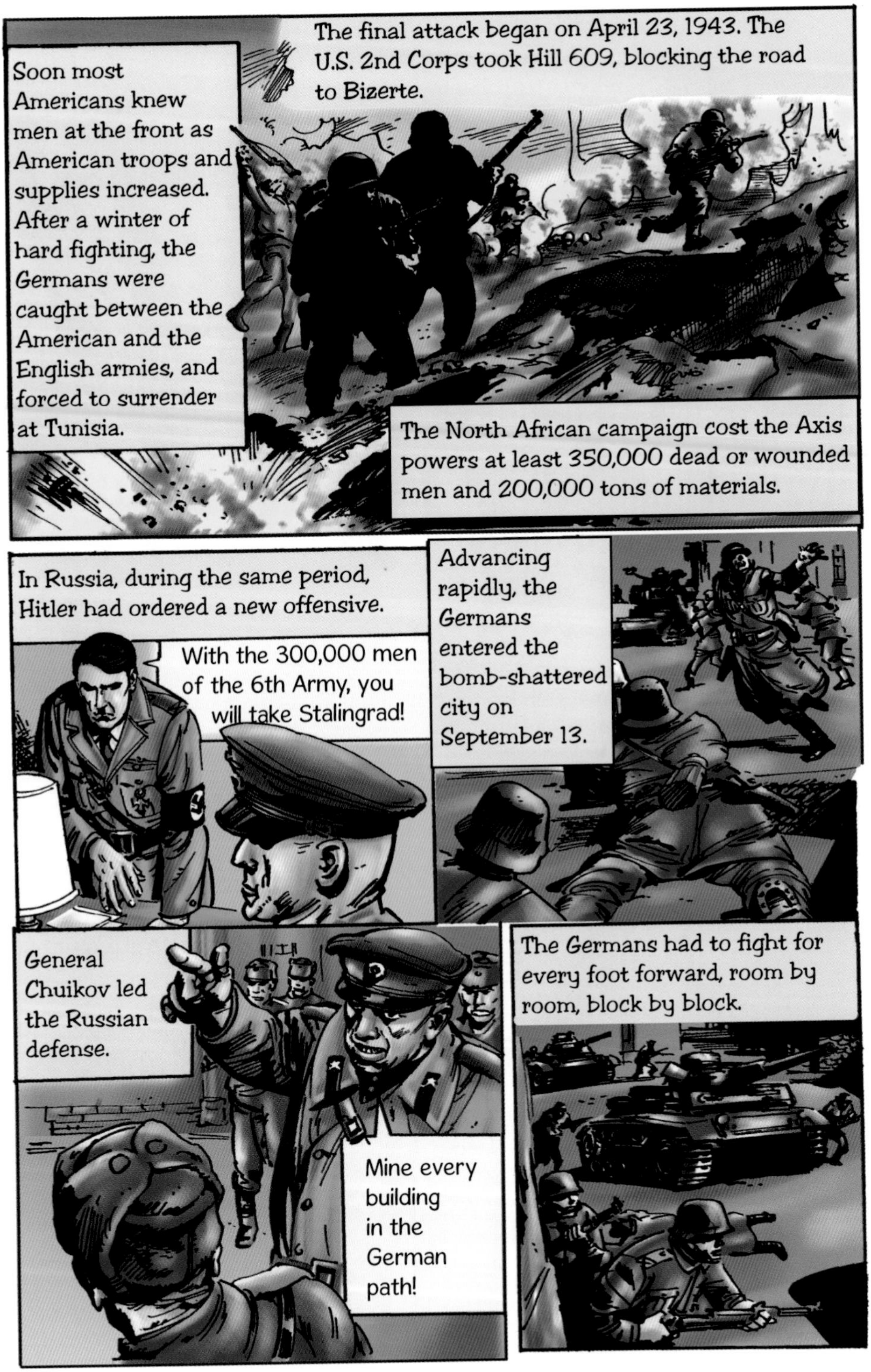
Soon most Americans knew men at the front as American troops and supplies increased. After a winter of hard fighting, the Germans were caught between the American and the English armies, and forced to surrender at Tunisia.
The final attack began on April 23, 1943. The U.S. 2nd Corps took Hill 609, blocking the road to Bizerte.
The North African campaign cost the Axis powers at least 350,000 dead or wounded men and 200,000 tons of materials.
In Russia, during the same period, Hitler had ordered a new offensive.
With the 300,000 men of the 6th Army, you will take Stalingrad!
Advancing rapidly, the Germans entered the bomb-shattered city on September 13.
General Chuikov led the Russian defense.
Mine every building in the German path!
The Germans had to fight for every foot forward, room by room, block by block.

On November 19, with large reinforcements, the Russians counterattacked, encircling the German army and cutting its supply lines. On January 31, 1943, General Paulus surrendered with the 91,000 starving survivors of his army.

In North Africa, in Russia, the Allied forces had finally won victories. But to counterattack the Japanese on land meant jungle fighting. The Japanese were sure the Americans could not stand that.

In Washington, the generals planned strategy.

The one place where we can build up our forces and organize a counterattack is Australia.

Australia and New Zealand are raising new units. And we're moving in troops, planes, and supplies very rapidly.

Then there was bad news.

The Japanese are building an air base on Guadalcanal, close to Australia. With land-based bombers from there, they can cut our supply lines and prevent our build-up.

Then we must take Guadalcanal!

On August 7, after a three-hour bombardment of the island, combat troops of the 1st Marines made an amphibious landing on Guadalcanal.

Quickly, the marines seized their first objective, the unfinished airstrip, and named it Henderson Field.

It began easily, but before ending the Guadalcanal campaign would include six separate naval battles, and a jungle fight that would last for eight months.

Hacking their way through dense jungles inhabited by all kinds of insects and snakes ...

Learning to spot Japanese snipers in the tree branches ...

Holding difficult positions against superior Japanese forces ...

In this way the marines eventually drove the Japanese from Guadalcanal, as they would later from many Pacific islands.

From Africa, Allied troops moved across the Mediterranean to Sicily, defeating the German and Italian troops there by the end of summer. From Sicily, they moved to Italy itself, for the first Allied landings in Europe.

En route to Italy, the troops heard a broadcast.

Listen! It's General Eisenhower!

The Italian government has surrendered its forces unconditionally.

Hey! We won't have to fight!

But the Germans had rushed crack troops to Italy to defend it. On the Salerno beaches, Allied troops were pinned down by artillery fire, and bombed by the Luftwaffe.

This was a warning of things to come. All winter the Allied troops fought their way up the Italian boot, through rugged mountain country. German artillery was mounted on every ridge. Rain, mud, snow, and cold added to the misery. As the Germans retreated, they destroyed bridges over all the rivers. It was not until June 4, 1944, that the Allies reached Rome.

Rome was the first European capital to be freed from the Nazis. The Italians greeted the Allies with enthusiasm.

Two days later the announcement came that Allied forces under General Eisenhower had landed in France.

In 1943, in Algiers at a Christmas party with his staff, General Eisenhower received special orders.

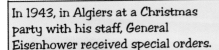

I have been made supreme commander of Operation Overlord.

The invasion of France! It will be in good hands, sir!

Flying to England, Eisenhower took charge of the invasion build-up, which turned all southern England into an armed camp.

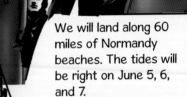

We will land along 60 miles of Normandy beaches. The tides will be right on June 5, 6, and 7.

On June 5, 1944, they were ready to go: three million Allied soldiers, sailors, and airmen; 4,000 ships; 20,111 vehicles; 1,500 tanks; 12,000 planes. But the weather was bad.

Such an operation could not be completely secret. Across the Channel the Germans knew it was coming, but not exactly where or when.

I will drive back to Berlin to celebrate my wife's birthday and to see Hitler.

Erwin Rommel was in charge of the German forces.

The first 24 hours will decide the outcome! But the weather is bad, they won't come now.

The forecasters predicted a short spell of clear weather. Eisenhower decided to go. By 5:30 a.m. on June 6, men and tanks were swarming ashore in Normandy.

The Germans fought back from their fortified positions, but by nightfall, 155,000 Allied troops were ashore.

Capturing Cherbourg after a three-week siege, the Americans found it reduced to ruins by the Germans.

As the Allied armies advanced, the people of Paris rose against their captors. On August 25, free French units entered the city and received the surrender of the German commander.

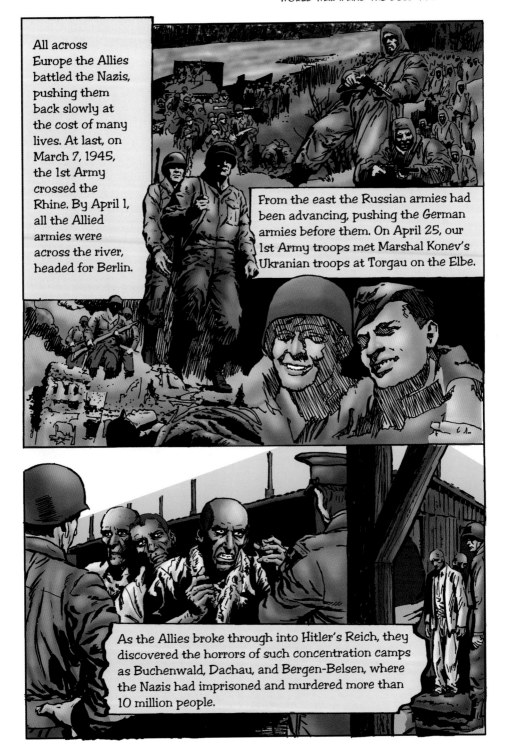

All across Europe the Allies battled the Nazis, pushing them back slowly at the cost of many lives. At last, on March 7, 1945, the 1st Army crossed the Rhine. By April 1, all the Allied armies were across the river, headed for Berlin.

From the east the Russian armies had been advancing, pushing the German armies before them. On April 25, our 1st Army troops met Marshal Konev's Ukranian troops at Torgau on the Elbe.

As the Allies broke through into Hitler's Reich, they discovered the horrors of such concentration camps as Buchenwald, Dachau, and Bergen-Belsen, where the Nazis had imprisoned and murdered more than 10 million people.

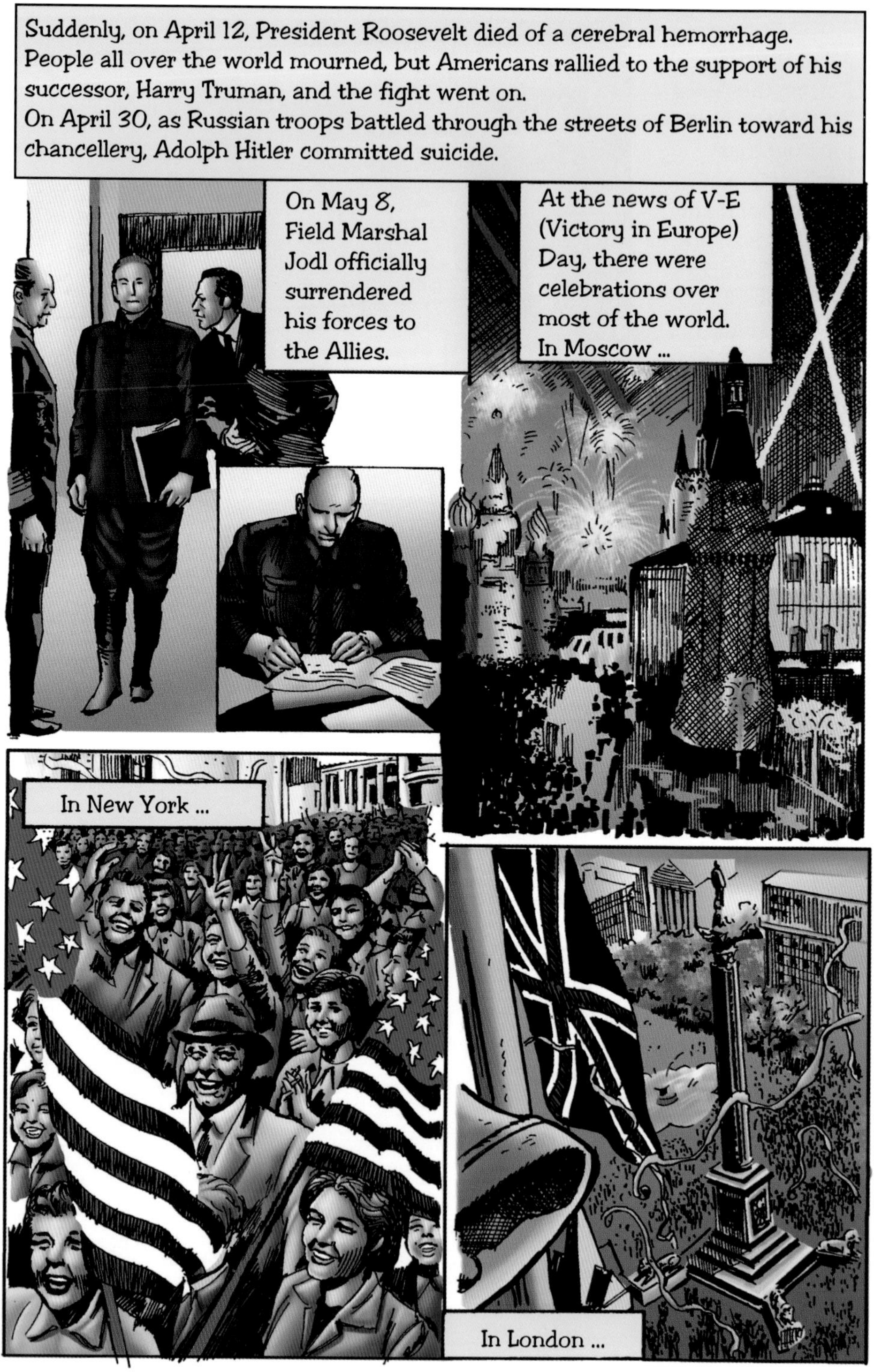
Suddenly, on April 12, President Roosevelt died of a cerebral hemorrhage. People all over the world mourned, but Americans rallied to the support of his successor, Harry Truman, and the fight went on.
On April 30, as Russian troops battled through the streets of Berlin toward his chancellery, Adolph Hitler committed suicide.
On May 8, Field Marshal Jodl officially surrendered his forces to the Allies.
At the news of V-E (Victory in Europe) Day, there were celebrations over most of the world. In Moscow ...
In New York ...
In London ...

But President Truman reminded the American people.

The victory is but half won. When the last naval Japanese division has surrendered unconditionally, only then will our job be done.

It was a long road back in the Pacific. Many naval battles were fought, many ships sank. It was October 1944 before the Americans fought their way back to the Philippines.

Albert Einstein, a refugee from Germany and one of history's greatest scientists, warned Roosevelt of the possibility of an atomic bomb. The Germans were working on it. The United States set up the Manhattan Project to try to manufacture an atomic bomb first.

It was here that the Japanese *kamikaze* suicide planes, loaded with high explosives, which the pilot would guide into its target, caused great damage.

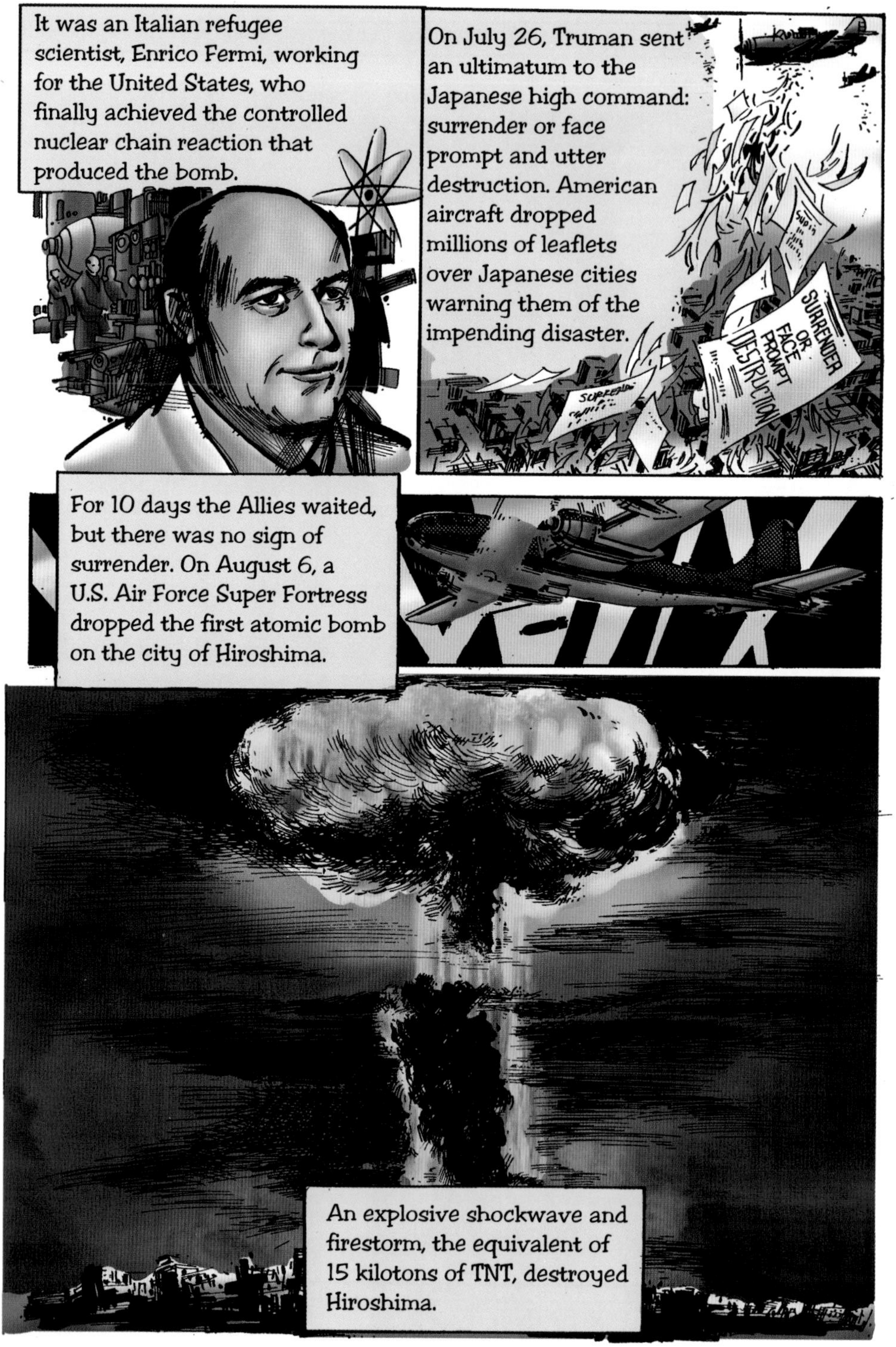
It was an Italian refugee scientist, Enrico Fermi, working for the United States, who finally achieved the controlled nuclear chain reaction that produced the bomb.
On July 26, Truman sent an ultimatum to the Japanese high command: surrender or face prompt and utter destruction. American aircraft dropped millions of leaflets over Japanese cities warning them of the impending disaster.
SURRENDER OR FACE PROMPT DESTRUCTION
For 10 days the Allies waited, but there was no sign of surrender. On August 6, a U.S. Air Force Super Fortress dropped the first atomic bomb on the city of Hiroshima.
An explosive shockwave and firestorm, the equivalent of 15 kilotons of TNT, destroyed Hiroshima.

Meantime, men had been planning for the peace. In June 1945, delegates from 50 countries met in San Francisco to organize the United Nations.

The day before he died, President Roosevelt dictated the draft of a speech.

The mere conquest of our enemies is not enough. Today we are faced with the fact that, if civilization is to survive, we must cultivate the science of human relationships—the ability of all peoples to live together in the same world, at peace.

The Japanese high command made no move. On August 9, a second bomb was dropped on Nagasaki. On August 15, the Emperor addressed the Japanese people.

We have resolved to pave the way for a grand peace for all the generations to come.

On September 2, on the battleship *Missouri*, Japanese envoys signed an unconditional surrender.